UNIT 11
Cycles

INTER·ACTIVE

Mathematics

Activities & Investigations

GLENCOE
McGraw-Hill

New York, New York   Columbus, Ohio   Mission Hills, California   Peoria, Illinois

Send all inquiries to:
Glencoe/McGraw-Hill
936 Eastwind Drive
Westerville, OH 43081

ISBN: 0-02-824513-X (Student Resource Book)
ISBN: 0-02-824495-8 (Teacher's Edition)

4 5 6 7 8 9 10 11 12   071/043   02 01 00 99 98 97

CONTRIBUTORS INTERACTIVE MATHEMATICS

Each of the Consultants read all 18 units while each Reviewer read one unit. The Consultants and Reviewers gave suggestions for improving the Student Resource Books, Teacher's Editions, Cooperative Group Cards, Posters, and Transparencies. The Writers wrote the Student Diversity Strategies that appear in the Teacher's Edition.

CONSULTANTS

Dr. Judith Jacobs, *Units 1-18*
  *Director, Center for Science
    and Mathematics Education
  California State
    Polytechnic University
  Pomona, California*

Dr. Cleo M. Meek, *Units 1-18*
  *Mathematics Consultant,
  Retired
  North Carolina Dept. of
    Public Instruction
  Raleigh, North Carolina*

Beatrice Moore-Harris,
  *Units 1-18
  College Board Equity 2000
    Site Coordinator
  Fort Worth Independent
    School District
  Fort Worth, Texas*

Deborah J. Murphy, *Units 1-18*
  *Mathematics Teacher
  Killingsworth Jr. High School,
  ABC Unified School District
  Cerritos, California*

Javier Solorzano, *Units 1-18*
  *Mathematics Teacher
  South El Monte High School
  South El Monte, California*

WRITERS

**Student Diversity
Teacher's Edition**

Dr. Gilbert J. Cuevas
  *Professor of Mathematics
    Education
  University of Miami
  Coral Gables, Florida*

Sally C. Mayberry, *Ed.D.*
  *Assistant Professor
    Mathematics/Science
    Education
  St. Thomas University
  Miami, Florida*

REVIEWERS

John W. Anson, *Unit 11*
  *Mathematics Teacher
  Arroyo Seco Junior High
    School
  Valencia, California*

Laura Beckwith, *Unit 13*
  *Mathematics Department
    Chairperson
  William James Middle School
  Fort Worth, Texas*

Betsy C. Blume, *Unit 6*
  *Vice Principal/
    Director of Curriculum
  Valleyview Middle School
  Denville, New Jersey*

James F. Bohan, *Unit 11*
  *Mathematics K-12 Program
    Coordinator
  Manheim Township School
    District
  Lancaster, Pennsylvania*

Dr. Carol Fry Bohlin, *Unit 14*
  *Director, San Joaquin Valley
    Mathematics Project
  Associate Professor,
    Mathematics Education
  California State University,
    Fresno
  Fresno, California*

David S. Bradley, *Unit 9*
  *Mathematics
    Teacher/Department
    Chairperson
  Jefferson Jr. High
  Kearns, Utah*

Dr. Diane Briars, *Unit 9*
  *Mathematics Specialist
  Pittsburgh City Schools
  Pittsburgh, Pennsylvania*

INTERACTIVE MATHEMATICS AUTHORS

KAY McCLAIN

"Building conceptual understanding in mathematics challenges us to re-define what it means to know and do mathematics. This program was developed to allow teachers to become facilitators of learning while students explore and investigate mathematics — strengthening their understanding and stimulating interest."

Kay McClain

**Doctoral Candidate
George Peabody College
Vanderbilt University
Nashville, Tennessee**
Author of Unit 9, Co-author of Unit 14

BARNEY MARTINEZ

"Students learn mathematics best when their teacher enables them to become actively involved in worthwhile mathematical investigations. Students should be encouraged to interact with each other. Then, through their collaborative efforts, students build their own understanding of mathematics."

Barney Martinez

**Mathematics Teacher
Jefferson High School
Daly City, California**
Co-Author of Unit 12

LINDA DRITSAS

"This program is designed to encourage students to be creative and inventive, while gaining mathematical power. Open-ended situations and investigations provide the setting that allows students to work at varying depths, while nurturing their natural curiosity to learn."

Linda Dritsas

**Mathematics Coordinator
Fresno Unified School District
Fresno, California**
Author of Unit 4, Co-author of Unit 12

Kay McClain received her B.A. from Auburn University and her Educational Specialist degree from the University of Montevallo in Montevallo, Alabama. While a teacher at Mountain Brook Middle School in Birmingham, she received the Presidential Award for Excellence in the Teaching of Mathematics in the state of Alabama. Ms. McClain is a Woodrow Wilson fellow and a member of the National Council of Teachers of Mathematics. She regularly conducts teacher in-service workshops and is a frequent speaker at local, state, and national mathematics education conferences. She is also an author of middle school mathematics instructional materials.

Barney Martinez received his B.S. in mathematics from The University of San Francisco and is an instructor of pre-service mathematics teachers at the College of Notre Dame in Belmont, California. Mr. Martinez currently serves on the Mathematics Development Team of the California Department of Education and the Pursuing Excellence Revision Advisory Committee. He is a member of the National Council of Teachers of Mathematics and is very active as a speaker and workshop leader at professional development conferences.

Linda Dritsas received her B.A. and M.A. from California State University at Fresno. She taught middle school mathematics for many years and, for two years, taught mathematics at California State University at Fresno. Ms. Dritsas has been the Central Section President of the California Mathematics Council and is a member of the National Council of Teachers of Mathematics and the Association for Supervision and Curriculum Development. She frequently conducts mathematics teacher in-service workshops and is an author of numerous mathematics instructional materials, including those for middle school students and teachers.

DAVID FOSTER

"The national goal is to develop mathematical power for all students. My vision for learning mathematics includes a student-oriented classroom culture, where students are taking charge of their own learning and are actively engaged in a curriculum that reflects today's world, not the mathematics of 150 years ago."

[signature: David Foster]

Former Teaching Consultant
  Middle Grades Mathematics
  Renaissance
Morgan Hill, California
Author of Units 1, 2, 5, 6, 7, 8, 10, 11, 13, 15, 16, 17, and 18

David Foster received his B.A. in mathematics from San Diego State University and has taken graduate courses in computer science at San Jose State University. He has taught mathematics and computer science for nineteen years at the middle school, high school, and college level. Mr. Foster is a founding member of the California Mathematics Project Advisory Committee and was Co-Director of the Santa Clara Valley Mathematics Project. Most recently, he has taken the position of Consulting Author for Glencoe Publishing. Mr. Foster is a member of many professional organizations including the National Council of Teachers of Mathematics and regularly conducts in-service workshops for teachers. He is also the author of a book on computer science.

SANDIE GILLIAM

"Many students only see mathematics as isolated number facts and formulas to memorize. By using this program, which incorporates the mathematics into a context of large, real-life units tied together with literature, science, and history, the middle school student can find meaning in the mathematics."

[signature: Sandie Gilliam]

Mathematics Teacher
San Lorenzo Valley High School
Felton, California
Co-author of Unit 14

Sandie Gilliam received her B.A. from San Jose State University and is a mentor teacher and instructor for the Monterey Bay Area Mathematics Project. She was a semi-finalist for the Presidential Award for Excellence in the Teaching of Mathematics in the state of California. Ms. Gilliam has served as a consultant for the California Department of Education and many local school districts and county offices of education. She is a member of the National Council of Teachers of Mathematics and is a frequent speaker at conferences and teacher in-service workshops. Ms. Gilliam was a writer and consultant for Glencoe's *Investigating Mathematics: An Interactive Approach.*

JACK PRICE

"This program is designed to help students become mathematically powerful as they develop problem-solving skills and self-reliance, as well as the ability to work well with others. At the same time, they will strengthen their basic skills and be exposed to new and exciting ideas in mathematics."

[signature: Jack Price]

Co-Director, Center for Science
  and Mathematics Education
California State Polytechnic
  University
Pomona, California
Author of Unit 3

Jack Price received his B.A. from Eastern Michigan University and his Doctorate in Mathematics Education from Wayne State University. Dr. Price has been active in mathematics education for over 40 years, 38 of those years at grades K through 12. In his current position, he teaches mathematics and methods courses for preservice teachers and consults with school districts on curriculum change. He is president of the National Council of Teachers of Mathematics, is a frequent speaker at professional conferences, conducts many teacher in-service workshops, and is an author of numerous mathematics instructional materials.

C O N T E N T S

UNIT 11

CYCLES
ALGEBRA PATTERNS

Interdisciplinary Applications

INTERACTIVE MATHEMATICS CONTRIBUTORS

Jackie Britton, *Unit 18*
Mathematics Teacher
V. W. Miller Intermediate
Pasadena, Texas

Sybil Y. Brown, *Unit 8*
Mathematics Teacher
Franklin Alternative Middle
School
Columbus, Ohio

Blanche Smith Brownley, *Unit 18*
Supervising Director of
Mathematics (Acting)
District of Columbia Public
Schools
Washington, D.C.

Bruce A. Camblin, *Unit 7*
Mathematics Teacher
Weld School District 6
Greeley, Colorado

Cleo Campbell, *Unit 15*
Coordinator of Mathematics,
K-12
Anne Arundel County
Public Schools
Annapolis, Maryland

Savas Carabases, *Unit 13*
Mathematics Supervisor
Camden City School District
Camden City, New Jersey

W. Karla Castello, *Unit 6*
Mathematics Teacher
Yerba Buena High School
San Jose, California

Diane M. Chase, *Unit 16*
Mathematics Teacher/
Department Chairperson
Pacific Jr. High School
Vancouver, Washington

Dr. Phyllis Zweig Chinn, *Unit 9*
Professor of Mathematics
Humboldt State University
Arcata, California

Nancy W. Crowther, *Unit 17*
Mathematics Teacher
Sandy Springs Middle School
Atlanta, Georgia

Regina F. Cullen, *Unit 13*
Supervisor of Mathematics
West Essex Regional Schools
North Caldwell, New Jersey

Sara J. Danielson, *Unit 17*
Mathematics Teacher
Albany Middle School
Albany, California

Lorna Denman, *Unit 10*
Mathematics Teacher
Sunny Brae Middle School
Arcata, California

Richard F. Dube, *Unit 4*
Mathematics Supervisor
Taunton High School
Taunton, Massachusetts

Mary J. Dubsky, *Unit 1*
Mathematics Curriculum
Specialist
Baltimore City Public Schools
Baltimore, Maryland

Dr. Leo Edwards, *Unit 5*
Director, Mathematics/
Science Education Center
Fayetteville State University
Fayetteville, North Carolina

Connie Fairbanks, *Unit 7*
Mathematics Teacher
South Whittier Intermediate
School
Whittier, California

Ana Marina C. Gomezgil, *Unit 15*
District Translator/Interpreter
Sweetwater Union
High School District
Chula Vista, California

Sandy R. Guerra, *Unit 9*
Mathematics Teacher
Harry H. Rogers Middle
School
San Antonio, Texas

Rick Hall, *Unit 4*
Curriculum Coordinator
San Bernardino County
Superintendent of Schools
San Bernardino, California

Carolyn Hansen, *Unit 14*
Instructional Specialist
Williamsville Central Schools
Williamsville, New York

Jenny Hembree, *Unit 8*
Mathematics Teacher
Shelby Co. East Middle
School
Shelbyville, Kentucky

Susan Hertz, *Unit 16*
Mathematics Teacher
Paul Revere Middle School
Houston, Texas

Janet L. Hollister, *Unit 5*
Mathematics Teacher
LaCumbre Middle School
Santa Barbara, California

Dorothy Nachtigall Hren, *Unit 12*
Mathematics Teacher/
Department Chairperson
Northside Middle School
Norfolk, Virginia

Grace Hutchings, *Unit 3*
Mathematics Teacher
Parkman Middle School
Woodland Hills, California

Lyle D. Jensen, *Unit 18*
Mathematics Teacher
Albright Middle School
Villa Park, Illinois

Robert R. Jones, *Unit 7*
Chief Consultant,
  Mathematics, Retired
North Carolina Department
  of Public Instruction
Raleigh, North Carolina

Mary Kay Karl, *Unit 3*
Mathematics Coordinator
Community Consolidated
  School District 54
Schaumburg, Illinois

Janet King, *Unit 14*
Mathematics Teacher
North Gulfport Junior High
Gulfport, Mississippi

Franca Koeller, *Unit 17*
Mathematics Mentor Teacher
Arroyo Seco Junior High
  School
Valencia, California

Louis La Mastro, *Unit 2*
Mathematics/Computer
  Science Teacher
North Bergen High School
North Bergen, New Jersey

Patrick Lamberti, *Unit 6*
Supervisor of Mathematics
Toms River Schools
Toms River, New Jersey

Dr. Betty Larkin, *Unit 14*
Mathematics Coordinator
K - 12
Lee County School District
Fort Myers, Florida

Ann Lawrence, *Unit 1*
Mathematics
  Teacher/Department
  Coordinator
Mountain Brook Jr. High
  School
Mountain Brook, Alabama

Catherine Louise Marascalco,
  Unit 3
Mathematics Teacher
Southaven Elementary
  School
Southaven, Mississippi

Dr. Hannah Masterson, *Unit 10*
Mathematics Specialist
Suffolk Board of
  Cooperative Education
Dix Hills, New York

Betty Monroe Nelson, *Unit 8*
Mathematics Teacher
Blackburn Middle School
Jackson, Mississippi

Dale R. Oliver, *Unit 2*
Assistant Professor of
  Mathematics
Humboldt State University
Arcata, California

Carol A. Pudlin, *Unit 4*
Mathematics Teacher/
  Consultant
Griffiths Middle School
Downey, California

Diane Duggento Sawyer,
  Unit 15
Mathematics Chairperson
Exeter Area Junior High
Exeter, New Hampshire

Donald W. Scheuer, Jr., *Unit 12*
Mathematics Department
  Chairperson
Abington Junior High
Abington, Pennsylvania

Linda S. Shippey, *Unit 8*
Mathematics Teacher
Bondy Intermediate School
Pasadena, Texas

Barbara Smith, *Unit 1*
Mathematics Supervisor,
  K-12
Unionville-Chadds Ford
  School District
Kennett Square, Pennsylvania

Stephanie Z. Smith, *Unit 14*
Project Assistant
University of Wisconsin-
  Madison
Madison, Wisconsin

Dora M. Swart, *Unit 11*
Mathematics Teacher
W. F. West High School
Chehalis, Washington

Ciro J. Tacinelli, Sr., *Unit 8*
Curriculum Director:
  Mathematics
Hamden Public Schools
Hamden, Connecticut

Kathy L. Terwelp, *Unit 12*
K-8 Mathematics Supervisor
Summit Public Schools
Summit, New Jersey

Marty Terzieff, *Unit 18*
Secondary Math Curriculum
  Chairperson
Mead Junior High School
Mead, Washington

Linda L. Walker, *Unit 18*
Mathematics Teacher
Cobb Middle School
Tallahassee, Florida

CYCLES

Looking Ahead

In this unit, you will see how mathematics can be used to answer questions about number patterns and operations. You will experience:

▶ solving problems involving time measurement

▶ exploring clock arithmetic

▶ solving problems using cyclical patterns

▶ using technology to collect data and solve problems

▶ converting between standard and base-ten time systems

Did You Ever Wonder?

What do mathematics and embroidery have to do with each other? Turn the page and see how Susan Behm of Westminster, Colorado, combines the two!

Teens in the News

Featuring: **Susan E. Behm**
Age: **19**
Hometown: **Westminster, Colorado**
Career Goal: **Business Management**
Interests: **Computers,
  playing the accordion**

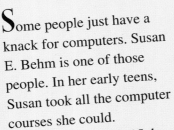

Some people just have a knack for computers. Susan E. Behm is one of those people. In her early teens, Susan took all the computer courses she could.

When Susan was 15, her mother was working for a company that makes embroidery machines. Her mother brought home a demonstration machine. Susan was fascinated by this sewing machine that was attached to a computer! Susan could type into the computer any size design and custom specifications she wanted on a shirt, sweater, or jacket. The computer would read her specs into a design program and then into the sewing machine.

Susan really got hooked on creating her own customized designs. Now her mother works for her, and they run **Suzie Q's Embroidery** out of the basement of their home!

Susan uses what she learned in geometry to help create her designs. She determines the size of the design and finds the exact center of it to place it on the material. She calculates the per-piece cost of each item as well as taxes.

Susan wants to expand her business. She plans to have a larger shop and hire full-time employees. She also intends to purchase her own digitizing machine. Then she could create and program her own designs onto computer disks. The next time you buy an item with customized lettering and designs, look for **Suzie Q's Embroidery** label.

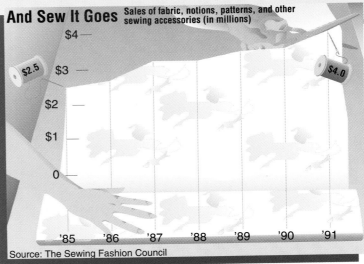

And Sew It Goes Sales of fabric, notions, patterns, and other sewing accessories (in millions)

$4
$2.5
$3
$4.0
$2
$1
0

'85 '86 '87 '88 '89 '90 '91

Source: The Sewing Fashion Council

Team Project

Designs in Time

Suzie Q's Embroidery has hired you to create a customized design. This design will appear on shirts, jackets, and sweaters. Your design should appeal to the students at your school.

The computers at **Suzie Q's Embroidery** read stitch commands in the form of ordered pairs. The machines can make stitches in multiples of $\frac{1}{16}$-inch lengths, from $\frac{1}{16}$ inch to 1 inch.

The machines can make 10 stitches per second.

Create your design and "program" the computer. How long will it take the machine to produce your design?

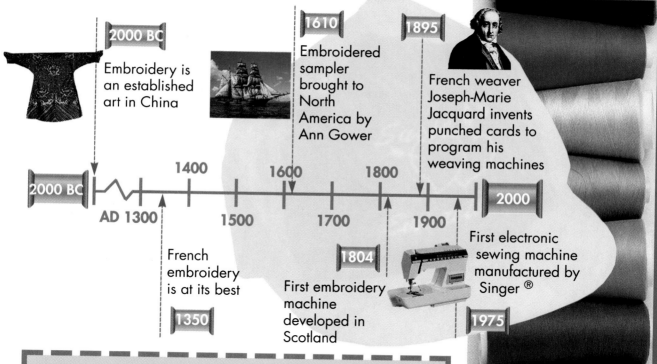

2000 BC — Embroidery is an established art in China

1610 — Embroidered sampler brought to North America by Ann Gower

1895 — French weaver Joseph-Marie Jacquard invents punched cards to program his weaving machines

1350 — French embroidery is at its best

1804 — First embroidery machine developed in Scotland

1975 — First electronic sewing machine manufactured by Singer ®

Timeline: 2000 BC, AD 1300, 1400, 1500, 1600, 1700, 1800, 1900, 2000

For more information

If you would like more information about forming your own company, contact:

JUNIOR ACHIEVEMENT, INC.
National Headquarters
One Education Way
Colorado Springs, Colorado
80906

You can learn more about the math Susan uses in her business by completing the following activities in this unit.

Setting the Scene

MATHEMATICS TOOLKIT

Many professions require the use of tools. This mathematics toolkit includes tools you may find useful as you study this unit. At times you may feel lost or not know where to begin when presented with a problem situation. Take time to read this toolkit to see the different mathematical tools and problem-solving strategies the characters in the script used. You don't need to wait until your teacher tells you to use a mathematical tool. Instead, if it seems like it might help, try it.

Narrator: Isabel, Teresa, John, Mario, Jason, and Lynn are officers in the Ecology Club at Lincoln Middle School. They are having a meeting in January. Isabel is the president of the club, and Jason is the treasurer.

Isabel: Now it's time for the treasurer's report. Jason, are you ready?

Jason: Well, sort of.

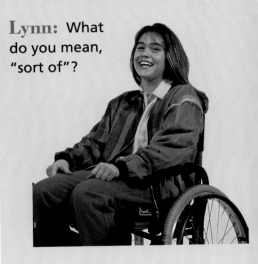

Lynn: What do you mean, "sort of"?

Jason: It means I kinda messed up.

Mario: Does that mean we're broke?

Jason: I don't know. I'm having trouble making sense of all these numbers.

John: Do you have the amounts we spent on the recycling bins for the school?

Teresa: How about the money we earned each week from collecting aluminum cans?

Jason: Yeah, yeah. I've kept good records. I'm just confused about what to do with all these numbers.

Isabel: We need to figure this out so we know how much we can spend for Arbor Day and Earth Week.

Mario: So far we have been spending money out of the student activities fund. We might really be broke.

John: I know. We'd better figure this out or we could be paying money out of our own pockets. They might not let us graduate.

Teresa: Don't panic. Jason has everything we have earned and spent listed here.

Narrator: Below is the list of all income (earnings) and expenditures (expenses) for this year.

John: Wow, look at this list! I can't tell whether we owe money or not.

Lynn: We need to figure it out quickly, so we know how much money we have.

Date	Transaction	Amount
9/10	Earnings from aluminum can weekly recycling	15.31
9/17	Earnings from aluminum can weekly recycling	12.78
9/21	Purchased 5 recycling bins for school	55.00
9/24	Earnings from aluminum can weekly recycling	17.56
10/1	Earnings from aluminum can weekly recycling	14.43
10/3	Purchased 3 recycling bins for school	33.00
10/8	Earnings from aluminum can weekly recycling	11.94
10/15	Earnings from aluminum can weekly recycling	13.89
10/17	Purchased 4 trees for community planting	26.40
10/22	Earnings from aluminum can weekly recycling	14.22
10/24	Purchased supplies for Halloween party	36.12
10/29	Earnings from aluminum can weekly recycling	15.92
11/5	Earnings from aluminum can weekly recycling	12.87
11/12	Earnings from aluminum can weekly recycling	14.66
11/15	Purchased 6 trees for community planting	39.60
11/19	Earnings from aluminum can weekly recycling	13.20
11/25	Earnings from aluminum can weekly recycling	8.17
12/2	Earnings from aluminum can weekly recycling	16.23
12/5	Purchased 7 recycling bins for school	77.00
12/9	Earnings from aluminum can weekly recycling	14.94
12/16	Earnings from aluminum can weekly recycling	13.33
12/20	Purchased supplies for holiday party	68.45
12/23	Earnings from aluminum can weekly recycling	12.74
1/14	Earnings from aluminum can weekly recycling	16.23

Isabel: Remember, we planned to spend $40 to buy three more trees for Arbor Day and about $100 for Earth Week.

Mario: Yeah, and we were also hoping to buy another six recycling bins for the areas we don't have covered on campus.

Teresa: I think we will have enough for all of those things. Remember we collect aluminum cans and turn them in each week for cash. School doesn't let out until the second week in June.

Lynn: The worst case is that we will have to hold another fundraiser so that we don't go bankrupt!

John: Let's stop talking and start figuring this out right now.

Stop the Script!
Determine the Ecology Club's account balance. Also, determine a budget for the remainder of the school year. Be prepared to share your budget with the rest of the class.

Narrator: The six officers start figuring out the account balance.

Mario: I know an easy way to figure out our balance using rational numbers and a calculator.

John: Rational numbers?

Mario: You know, fractions, decimals and signed numbers. You use + and −.

Lynn: That's right. Use a + sign for the money we earn and a − sign for the amount we spend.

Teresa: So our list would look like this?

Narrator: Teresa shows the group the list at the right.

Mario: Yeah, you got it. Just put a + in front of the amounts we earned and a − in front of the amounts we spent.

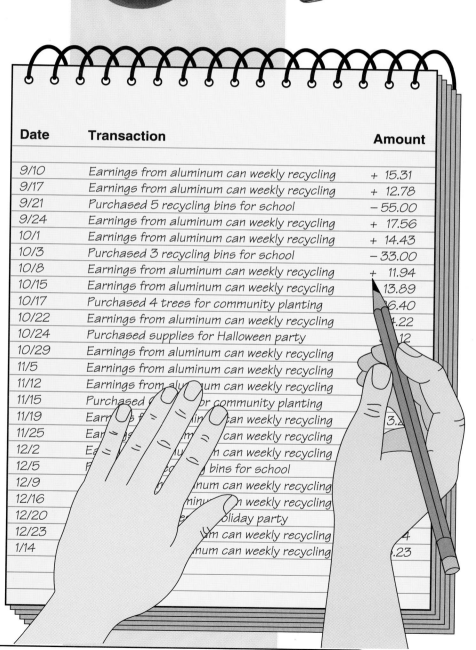

Date	Transaction	Amount
9/10	Earnings from aluminum can weekly recycling	+ 15.31
9/17	Earnings from aluminum can weekly recycling	+ 12.78
9/21	Purchased 5 recycling bins for school	− 55.00
9/24	Earnings from aluminum can weekly recycling	+ 17.56
10/1	Earnings from aluminum can weekly recycling	+ 14.43
10/3	Purchased 3 recycling bins for school	− 33.00
10/8	Earnings from aluminum can weekly recycling	+ 11.94
10/15	Earnings from aluminum can weekly recycling	13.89
10/17	Purchased 4 trees for community planting	6.40
10/22	Earnings from aluminum can weekly recycling	.22
10/24	Purchased supplies for Halloween party	12
10/29	Earnings from aluminum can weekly recycling	
11/5	Earnings from aluminum can weekly recycling	
11/12	Earnings from aluminum can weekly recycling	
11/15	Purchased for community planting	
11/19	Earnings from aluminum can weekly recycling	3.
11/25	Earnings from aluminum can weekly recycling	
12/2	Earnings from aluminum can weekly recycling	
12/5	bins for school	
12/9	aluminum can weekly recycling	
12/16	aluminum can weekly recycling	
12/20	holiday party	
12/23	aluminum can weekly recycling	4
1/14	aluminum can weekly recycling	.23

Jason: So how does that work with a calculator?

Lynn: Easy. First clear the calculator. Then press the key for the sign and type in the number. Then enter the next sign and the next number, over and over again until you get to the end of the list. At the end, you press ⌹.

John: So how does the calculator do it? I mean, what is the calculator actually doing?

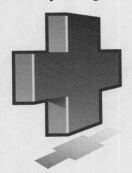

Isabel: It's just adding up the numbers.

Jason: Adding? Don't those minus signs mean subtract and the plus signs mean add? How can you subtract a larger number from a smaller number?

Mario: When you combine rational numbers, you can think of it as adding and subtracting. Really it is just moving along a number line.

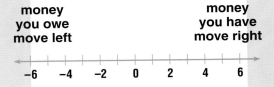

money you owe move left | money you have move right

–6 –4 –2 0 2 4 6

For example, suppose you have $5 and you want to buy something that costs $9. You start with 5 and move back nine (–9). That means you are $4 short.

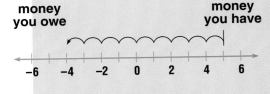

money you owe | money you have

–6 –4 –2 0 2 4 6

Jason: So if you buy something for $10, then you make it a negative number, –10, and you move to the left 10 spaces on the number line?

Lynn: Yes, and if you start out owing somebody like your Mom $3, you start at −3. Suppose you get paid $7. Then you move to the right 7 spaces. You can pay your Mom back and have $4 left.

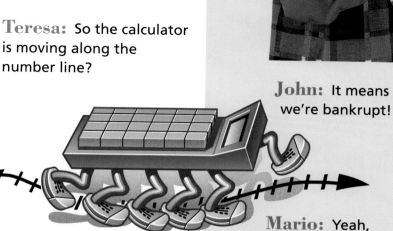

money you owe   money you have

Teresa: So the calculator is moving along the number line?

Jason: What does that mean?

John: It means we're bankrupt!

Teresa: You panic too much. The student activities fund will cover us for now. We still have five more months of income from our recycling projects.

Lynn: Well, kinda. Of course, the calculator does it electronically. We could do it by hand, although it would take a lot longer.

Mario: Yeah, we're almost $100 in the hole!

Jason: How much will that be?

John: Hey, that's what technology is for! Isabel, just use the calculator.

Isabel: Let's figure out what our average income is each week.

Isabel: Okay, I just entered the last number and I'm pressing the equal sign, ⊟ . There, we get −97.15.

Lynn: Okay, I'll find the mean by adding up all the income and dividing by the number of weeks.

15.31 $+$ 12.78 $+$ 17.56 $+$ 14.43 $+$ 11.94 $+$ 13.89 $+$ 14.22 $+$ 15.92 $+$ 12.87 $+$ 14.66 $+$ 13.20 $+$ 8.17 $+$ 16.23 $+$ 14.94 $+$ 13.33 $+$ 12.74 $+$ 16.23 $=$ *238.42*

Our total income is $238.42 and there were 17 weeks.

238.42 $\div$ 17 $=$ *14.024706*

So, we make an average of about $14 per week.

John: How many weeks of school are left?

Jason: Here, I'll count them. There is a calendar on the wall. Not counting spring break, there are 19 more weeks of school.

Mario: Okay, 19 weeks times $14 per week makes $266. We owe $97.15. I'll combine –97.15 with +266.

$-$ 97.15 $+$ 266 $=$ *168.85*

We should have $168.85 by the time school is out for summer.

Isabel: So, we can use $168.85 for Arbor Day and Earth Week?

John: Can we buy any more recycling bins?

Teresa: We can't keep spending money that we don't have yet.

Lynn: We need to make a new budget before we can spend any more money. Jason, here, I'll show you how to set it up.

You make two different columns. One is for income (earnings) and one is for expenditures (expenses). First the income:

Narrator: Lynn shows the following list to Jason.

Lynn: Yes, that's right, but remember it is still an estimate. Now for the expenditures, we do a similar thing.

Narrator: Lynn creates the list at the right and shows it to Jason.

Expenditures	
Spend to date:	−335.57
Earth Day:	−100.00
Arbor Day:	−40.00
Total expenditures:	−475.57

Income	
Earned to date:	238.42
Estimated earnings:	266.00
Total income:	504.42

Jason: I get it. You have listed all the money we have earned so far from recycling and what we estimate we will make over the next five months. So, the $504.42 is what we will make over the entire year.

Jason: I see. The negative number –335.57 means we spent that amount so far this year. For Earth Week and Arbor Day we expect to spend those other amounts listed, –100.00 and –40.00.

John: And the –475.57 is the amount of money we expect to spend this year.

Lynn: Right. So now we find the balance by adding or combining those two totals. Using the calculator, we get our balance.

504.42 ⊟ 475.57 ⊟ *28.85*

John: Since the answer is positive, we won't be bankrupt!

Mario: I know. If the balance was negative we would owe the school money.

Teresa: I guess that means we can buy a couple of recycling bins.

Isabel: Not yet. Remember it's only an estimate. Maybe we should put some money in savings to be safe.

Jason: Good, I feel a lot better now about this budget.

John: We all should. I think we just lucked out. From now on we better keep up on this budget!

This concludes the Mathematics Toolkit. It included many mathematical tools for you to use throughout this unit. As you work through this unit, you should use these tools to help you solve problems. You may want to explain how to use these mathematical tools in your journal. Or you may want to create a toolkit notebook to add mathematical tools you discover throughout this unit.

The Ice Age

You work for InGen Corporation, a biotechnology company in the silicon valley near San Jose, California. You have been assigned to work in their pre-historic investigation division.

This division of InGen works with archaeologists who recover fossils. InGen uses various methods such as carbon-14 dating and bone-structure analysis of the fossils to determine the length of time since an animal died.

A Neanderthal fossil has been found in a cave in La Chapelle-aux Saints, France. The InGen lab has just finished the carbon-14 dating and the bone-structure analysis of the fossil. Your division has been asked to determine the date and time the Neanderthal died and the date the Neanderthal was born. (Use the modern calendar.)

Use the InGen Corporation lab report in the Data Bank to complete your assignment. Write a group report. Be prepared to share the methods you used to arrive at the dates.

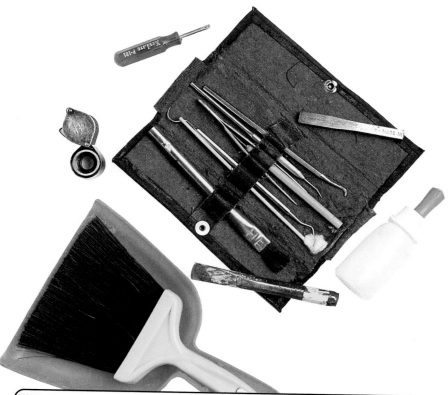

CALENDARS

If there are 365 days in a normal year, 366 days in a leap year (adding Feb. 29th to the calendar), and 7 days in a week, how many different calendars are there?

Two calendars are the same if every date of one calendar correspondingly falls on the same day of the week as the other calendar.

How many years pass before a calendar is repeated? Does it matter if the year you start with is leap year?

How many years does it take before each calendar is used once? Start counting with year 2001.

▶ FEBRUARY ◀

S	M	T	W	Th	F	S
■	■	■	■	1	2	3
4	5	6	7	8	9	10
11	12	13	14	15	16	17
18	19	20	21	22	23	24
25	26	27	28	29	■	■

How Long?

How long is 25 years, 12 weeks, 4 days, and 23 minutes?
State your answer in terms of seconds.
State your answer in terms of minutes.
State your answer in terms of days.
State your answer in terms of weeks.

How Old?

MENU station C

How old are you exactly?

In years?   In days?
In weeks?   In hours?
In minutes?   In seconds?
In seasons?   In months?
In decades?   In scores?
In centuries?

What problems occur in determining the above information?

Leaps

Ηow many Februarys since 1600 have had five Sundays? In what years of our modern calendar do New Year's Day and New Year's Eve fall on the same day of the week? Explain your answer.

MENU station E

Chime Times

A grandfather clock chimes 4 times when it is fifteen minutes after the hour, 8 times on the half-hour, 12 times when it is forty-five minutes after the hour, and on the hour it chimes 16 times plus it chimes the number of times equal to the hour. In one year, how many chimes are struck by the grandfather clock?

Game Clock

As a group, select one of the three game boards. Each pair should play the clock game several times. Record the sum of the number cubes for each move. Record the direction of each move by writing a positive sign (+) in front of the sum when you decide to go around the circle clockwise and a negative sign (−) in front of the sum when you decide to go around the circle counter-clockwise. In each game, you will create a list of signed whole numbers, or **integers**, to symbolize the size and direction of each move. You will use these lists later to analyze your moves.

After playing several games, determine who was able to finish a game in the fewest moves. How many moves? What was the greatest number of moves needed to finish a game? What is the average number of moves it took to finish a game in your group?

Once everyone in your group has played several games and discussed the results, try a different game circle. Play several games on that new circle as you did on the first. Did you find any difference between the two circle games?

Game Rules: The object of the game is to land on every numbered spot around the circle using as few moves as possible. Start at spot 0, but don't place a marker there. Roll three number cubes. The sum of the number cubes is the number of spaces you move. You may go around the circle in either direction (clockwise or counter-clockwise). Record the move. Move to the new location and place a marker there. If you have already visited that spot on the circle, move there but don't leave another marker. From the new location, repeat the process. The game ends when you have placed a marker on each spot on the circle.

Clock Five Game Board

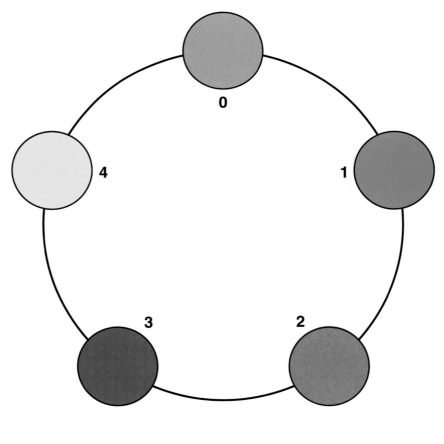

Exchange two or three circle game records with another pair. Replay the games they played. Determine if they could have finished the games in fewer moves by moving in the opposite direction on some of the turns.

Explain how you examined the games. If you found a faster method to finish a game, explain your method. If you think the other pair used the best strategy, show how the game could have been played to finish in more turns.

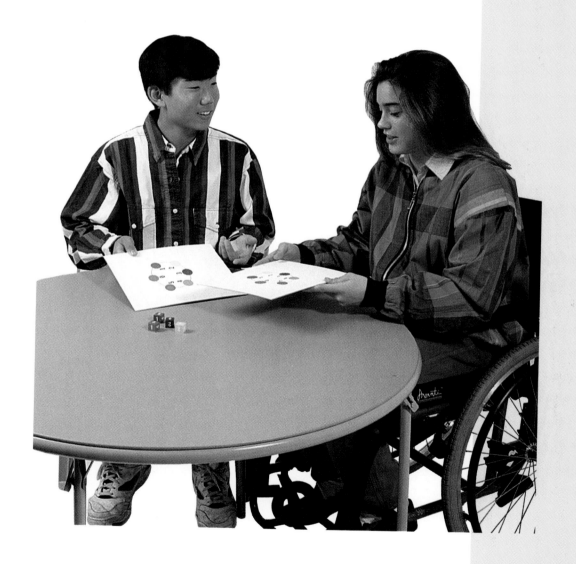

Select the records of the circle games you finished in both the most and least number of moves. Analyze those two games.

Longest game: Rearrange the order of the rolls to finish the game in the fewest number of moves. You cannot change the direction on a particular move; you can only change the order that the sums were rolled.

Shortest game: Rearrange the order of the rolls to finish the game in a different sequence. You cannot change the direction on a particular move; you can only change the order that the sums were rolled. Does the new game take more or fewer moves?

Explain how you analyzed the games. Did you find an easy method to solve these problems? What have you found out about the order of the rolls?

Back to the Future

*S*olve these problems in your group. Then each member of the group should write a note to another student describing the method(s) used to solve these problems.

- What time was it 7 hours ago if it is 5 o'clock now?
- It is 9 o'clock. What time was it 6 hours ago?
- It is 8 o'clock. What time will it be in 12 hours?
- What time was it 5 hours ago if it is 5 o'clock now?
- Today is Thursday. What day will it be in 5,000 days?
- Today is Monday. What day was it 11,352 days ago?
- This month is October. What month will it be in 30 months?
- This month is March. What month was it 300 months ago?
- This month is October. What month will it be in 3,003 days?

Dividing Time

Marty said to Doc, "So, we are going to travel back in time. What year did you set the Delorean for?"

"Ohhh, I forgot," said Doc.

"What do you mean?" exclaimed Marty. "We could be lost in a time continuum!"

"Well, what I remember is... if you divide that year by 2," Doc said, "you'll get a remainder of 1."

"Great Doc, that's every odd-numbered year. You gotta remember more!"

"Great Scott! I just got a jolt of 1.21 gigabytes of brain power. Now I know. If you divide the year by 3, 4, 5, 6, 7, or 9, you'll also get a remainder of 1."

"What about 8? If I divide by 8, do I get a remainder of 1?" asked Marty.

"No, Marty," replied Doc.

Marty said, "Alright Doc, that's it! Let's go."

What year are they off to? Be prepared to present your solution. Be creative with your presentation.

Times Square

Consider a clock with seven digits as shown below. Multiplication in a clock system is repeated addition as in regular arithmetic. For example, 3 times 4 means to start at 0 and count to 4 three times while moving around the clock in a clockwise direction. The result is 5.

Create a multiplication table for clock seven. Examine the multiplication table that you have created. Describe the features of the table. Are there patterns that appear? Explain.

Create two more clock multiplication tables for two other clock sizes. What have you discovered about clock multiplication?

Create a multiplication table in clock twelve. Explain patterns you found in creating the table. How did you determine the answer to each multiplication problem?

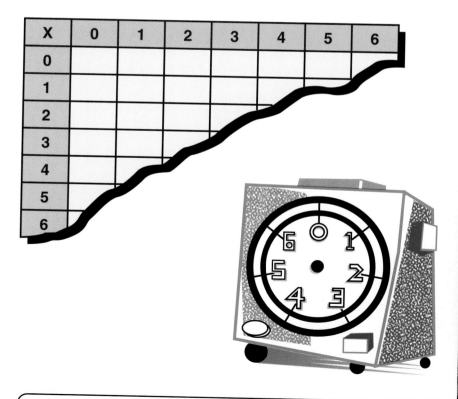

X	0	1	2	3	4	5	6
0							
1							
2							
3							
4							
5							
6							

Team Schedule

You are the student representative on the facility planning committee for Hoover Middle School. You have both a gym and a cafeteria on your campus. The dance team, basketball team, and wrestling team can use either of these two facilities for their events.

From November 1 through March 30, these teams have scheduled events.

- The dance team has an event scheduled for Monday, November 1, and every <u>third school day</u> after November 1 (Thursday, November 4; Tuesday, November 9; and so on).
- The basketball team has its first home game on Tuesday, November 2, and every <u>fourth school day</u> after that (Monday, November 8; Friday, November 12; and so on).
- The wrestling team has its first home match on Wednesday, November 3, and every <u>fifth school day</u> after that (Wednesday, November 10; Wednesday, November 17; and so on).

The Hoover school calendar includes the following holidays.

Thanksgiving: Thursday, November 25–Friday, November 26
Winter break: Monday, December 20–Friday, December 31
Dr. Martin Luther King Day: Monday, January 17
Presidents' Day: Monday, February 21

If it is not a leap year, are there any dates when all three teams have events on the same day?

Prepare a report for the planning committee. If there are conflicting dates, state the dates, explain how you determined those dates, and how you know there are not any more conflicting dates. If there are no conflicting dates, explain how you know for sure, and how you arrived at your answer.

Eccentric Clockmaker

An eccentric clockmaker built three different clocks.

The first clock was a five-minute clock designed with an alarm set to sound each time the hand reached the number 2 on the clock.

The second clock was a six-minute clock designed to sound each time the hand reached the number 3.

The third clock was a seven-minute clock designed to sound each time the hand reached the number 4.

The clockmaker started the clocks simultaneously one day, and each clock began to sound at its appropriate time. Was there a time when all three clocks sounded their alarms together? If so, tell when it occurred and explain why. If not, explain why not.

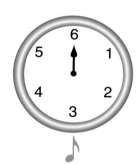

Spirolaterals

Spirolaterals are graphs made from sequences of numbers. The key to drawing any spirolateral is to follow this sequence of moves: UP-RIGHT-DOWN-LEFT. For example, to draw a 1, 2, 3 spirograph, first mark a starting point on graph paper. Next move up 1 space, then move right 2 spaces, and then move down 3 spaces. That completes one cycle. Continuing, you move left 1 space, move up 2 spaces, and move right 3 spaces.

A closed spirolateral is a spirolateral that will repeat itself after a number of cycles. In other words, after a certain number of cycles, a closed spirolateral will end in the same position and orientation where it originally began.

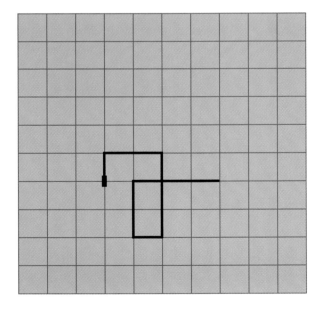

Using Graph Paper

A sequence with three terms forms an order—3 spirolaterals.

Draw a 4, 2, 1 and a 4, 3, 2 spirolateral.

Remember the key to drawing any spirolateral is UP-RIGHT-DOWN-LEFT.

On graph paper, draw an order-6 spirolateral like 4, 2, 6, 3, 7, 1. How does the sequence compare to an order-3 sequence? How does it differ?

On graph paper, draw other spirolaterals of your own. Record the sequence of numbers and describe each graph.

What are the characteristics of spirolaterals? Explain your findings.

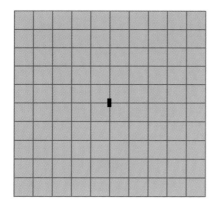
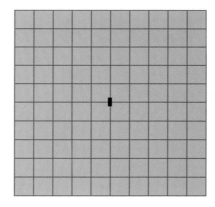

COMPUTER investigation

Using LOGO

Investigate spirolaterals using the computer. Type SPGRAPH 90 [1 2 3] in LOGO to draw a spirolateral with a sequence of 1,2,3. Make sure to type square brackets around the sequence of numbers and to separate the numbers in the sequence by *spaces*, not commas.

Your task is to discover properties of spirolaterals and to be able to generalize and predict the behavior of a spirolateral. Use the computer to draw and explore spirolaterals. Explain why you believe spirolaterals behave as they do.

Suppose the definition of a spirolateral is altered to allow the turning angle to change (for example, from 90° to 60°). How would that change the properties of closed spirolaterals? To explore these spirolaterals, substitute 60 for 90 in the program statement, i.e., SPGRAPH 60 [1 2 3]. Use isometric dot paper to draw a 60° spirolateral.

Write a report stating all the properties of spirolaterals that you have discovered during your investigations. Explain the process you used. Give specific examples to support your generalizations and draw diagrams to illustrate your findings.

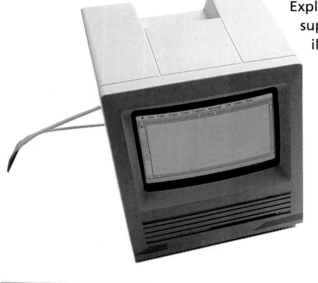

Metric Time

Suppose you invent a metric clock using the system below.
  1 day = 10 metric hours
  1 metric hour = 10 metric minutes
  1 metric minute = 10 metric seconds
  1 metric second = 10 metric miniseconds

  If a standard and a metric clock are started together (the standard clock at 12:00 midnight and the metric clock at 0), what is the time in our standard system when the metric clock registers 4 metric hours, 5 metric minutes, 6 metric seconds, and 7 metric miniseconds?

Suppose a metric calendar uses the system below.
  1 day = 1 metric day
  1 metric week = 10 metric days
  1 metric month = 10 metric weeks
  1 metric year = 10 metric months

If both calendars begin at 0 B.C., what was the metric calendar date on January 1, 1993? Explain how you arrived at your solution.

Jurassic Time

You work for InGen Corporation, a biotechnology company in the silicon valley. You have been assigned to work in their pre-historic investigation division. The division works with archaeologists in the field who recover dinosaur fossils. InGen uses various methods of dating to determine the length of time since a dinosaur died.

Your division has been assigned the task of determining a process for calculating the hour, day, month, and year a dinosaur died, given the length of time its fossil has existed. Use the modern calendar. Your process should be clear and work for any number of different time lengths. Explain why your process works.

Use three time measurements to demonstrate the accuracy of your process.

Prepare a presentation of your process for the InGen Corporation.

Galactic Time

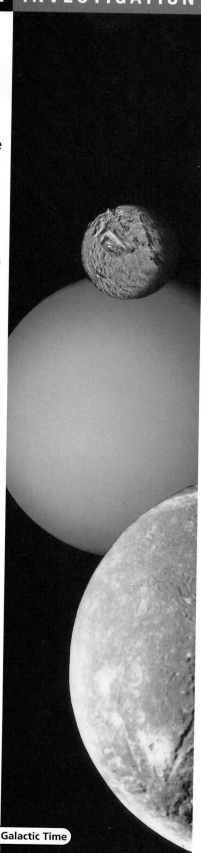

Linear, volume, temperature, and weight measurements have been converted from traditional measures to metric units. Standard units such as yards, miles, quarts, pounds, and degrees Fahrenheit have given way to meters, kilometers, liters, kilograms, and degrees Celsius, respectively. One standard measurement has not changed from its traditional roots. That measurement is "time." There are 60 minutes in an hour, 24 hours in a day, 7 days in a week, 52 weeks in a year, 12 months in a year, 365 or 366 days in a year, and so on.

With these different clock or calendar measurement sizes, calculating in time can be difficult and confusing. Many of the units such as the length of a day or the number of days in a year are related to nature. A day is defined as one revolution of Earth. A month originally was determined by one cycle of the moon, and a year is one rotation of Earth around the sun. This may make sense on Earth, but in space these measurements don't really apply.

- Do you think our time system is satisfactory?
- How might you change it?
- What would make sense if you were designing a system for space?

You work for NASA, and your group has been commissioned to design and implement a new system of "time" for space travel. Your new system can be based upon a number of factors. It can be metric or converted to a different clock system, such as 5, 7, or some other number. The system can be a combination of clock systems that might function well together. You should create a system that is reasonable, easy to calculate, adaptable, and practical.

Produce an original report with the following features:
- A complete explanation of your new time system, stating the name of each unit, its relationship to other units, and a means of conversion between standard time units and your new units
- A description and explanation of why you chose your system; why it is easier, reasonable, and useful; and how you might sell your new system to your superiors
- A design for a new clock and/or calendar that will use your system
- A conversion of the following dates and times to your new system:
  October 12, 1492
  July 4, 1776
  December 7, 1941
  November 22, 1963
  January 20, 1993 12:00 P.M.
  the date and time you were born

Selection and Reflection

Webster's Dictionary defines CYCLE as:

cy•cle 1 : an interval of time during which a sequence of a recurring succession of events or phenomena is completed 2 : a course or series of events or operations that recur regularly and usually lead back to the starting point 3: a circular or spiral arrangement 4 : a long period of time : age

Think about the title of this unit, *Cycles*, the definition, and the mathematics you learned in this unit.

- What have you learned about cycles in this unit?

- What do cycles have to do with mathematics?

- What mathematics did you use and learn while doing this unit? Use examples from several of the unit's activities in your explanation.

A Baffling Birthday

The Problem

Teresa is having a party at her house. The group is discussing birthdays and talking about planning parties. After listening for a while, Teresa says, "There is something interesting about my birthday. Two days ago I was 13, but next year I will turn 16." If Teresa is telling the truth, what kind of party is she having? When is her birthday?

The Problem

The *Winner's Circle*, a new TV game show, is coming out next fall. Contestants are selected randomly from the audience. The number of contestants is based on the number of spots in the circle on the stage, which varies with each show. At the announcer's signal, contestants race to the stage and stand on a spot in the circle. Starting with the red spot, the announcer says to the contestant on that spot "you stay." He continues to the next contestant on the right and says "you leave." To the third contestant, he says "you stay," and so on, around and around the circle, asking every other contestant to leave until just one contestant is left. This remaining contestant is the winner.

Suppose you are a contestant on *The Winner's Circle*. If there are 29 spots on the circle, where would you stand in relationship to the red spot to be the winner?

Extension Find a way to determine where to stand in a circle with any number of spots.

"I Am Thinking of a Number..."

250484762651838957
850857496707049474
4589578679690341
32488589360782753
6480009437348598
28078799575973459
56743783574759759 23

The Problem

What is the least positive number that you can divide by 7 and get a remainder of 4, divide by 8 and get a remainder of 5, and divide by 9 and get a remainder of 6?

74 456

27

?

15 120

The Problem

Shalonda is trying to outwit her brother Ben with a math question. He is allowed only 30 minutes to answer. Before asking the question, Shalonda and Ben agree that if he guesses correctly, then *she* will wash the dinner dishes, and if he guesses incorrectly, then *he* will wash the dishes. Shalonda asks the question: "If you use 8 as a factor 1,007 times, what would be the ones digit in the answer?" What number would Ben have to guess in order to get out of doing the dishes?

Sibling Rivalry

8X8X8X8X8X8X8X8X
8X8X8X8X8X8X8X8X
8X8X8X8X8X8X8X
8X8X8X8X8X8X8X
8X8X8X8X8X8X8X
8X8X8X8X8X8X8X
8X8X8X8X8X8X8X8X

Tick, Tock, A Broken Clock

1
9 3
6

The Problem

Mrs. Bluemel's grandfather clock is broken. The only time it will chime is when the minute hand and the hour hand are at right angles to each other. Each time it does chime, it chimes three times. In a 24-hour day, how many times does it chime?

The Problem

In the land of Spiro, everyone walks in order-3 spirolateral patterns. Within a family, each person has the same numbers in their spirolateral pattern, but the numbers may be in a different order. One day, Mrs. 2-4-5 plans to send one of her children to the grocery store and another one to the post office. If she has a child in every possible number combination of 2, 4, and 5, which child should she send to which store to make sure they get there and back?

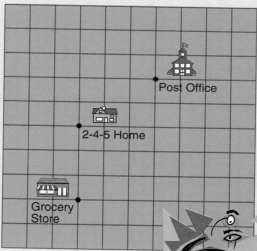

Post Office

2-4-5 Home

Grocery Store

Extension If the people of Spiro walked in order-4 spirolateral patterns, can you think of a problem they would encounter?

A Letter from Mars

The Problem

It is the 22nd century. A human settlement, called Mars City, has been established on the planet Mars. The people of Mars City use the metric, or base-ten, measure of time. The people on Earth, however, still use the standard measure of time.

The mayor of Mars City wants to write a letter to his sister in Los Angeles, California. If the date on Mars is 798 years, 9 weeks, and 9 days, what date should he put on the letter so his sister will know when he wrote it?

TABLE OF CONTENTS

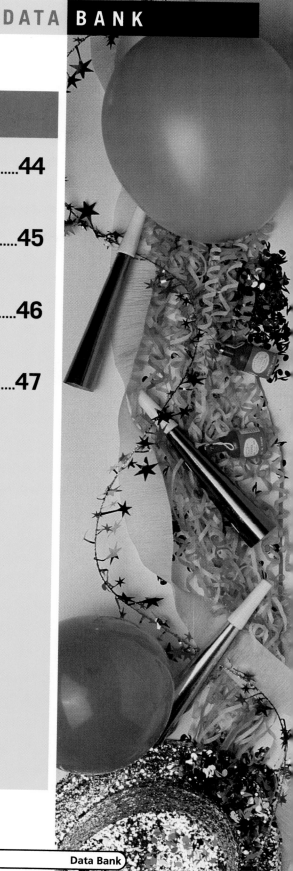

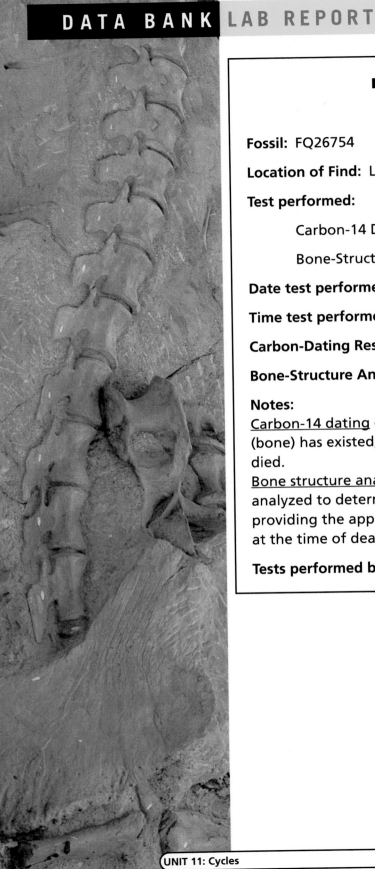

InGen Corporation

Lab Report

Fossil: FQ26754

Location of Find: La Chapelle-aux Saints, France

Test performed:

> Carbon-14 Dating

> Bone-Structure Analysis

Date test performed: Jan. 15, 1993

Time test performed: 12:00 noon

Carbon-Dating Results: 43,457.625 years

Bone-Structure Analysis Results: 24.25 years

Notes:

Carbon-14 dating determines the actual time a fossil (bone) has existed, starting from the time the creature died.

Bone structure analysis is a process in which a fossil is analyzed to determine the development of the bone, thus providing the approximate age of the once-living creature at the time of death.

Tests performed by: Dr. Bette Wright Knott

Time Conversions

1,000 nanoseconds = 1 second
100 milliseconds = 1 second
60 seconds = 1 minute
60 minutes = 1 hour
3,600 seconds = 1 hour
24 hours = 1 day
7 days = 1 week
365 days = 1 year
366 days = 1 leap year
52 weeks + 1 day = 1 year
12 months = 1 year
3 months = 1 season
4 seasons = 1 year
10 years = 1 decade
2 decades = 1 score
100 years = 1 century

Seasons

Winter is from December 21 to March 21.
Spring is from March 22 to June 20.
Summer is from June 21 to September 20.
Autumn is from September 21 to December 20.

Days in the Month

January has 31 days.

February has 28 or 29 days.

March has 31 days.

April has 30 days.

May has 31 days.

June has 30 days.

July has 31 days.

August has 31 days.

September has 30 days.

October has 31 days.

November has 30 days.

December has 31 days.

Leap Year occurs every four years on years divisible by 4. For example, 1992 was a leap year because 1992 divided by 4 has no remainder. The one exception occurs every odd turn of the century in years such as 1500, 1700, 1900, and so on. These are not leap years.

Type	Leap Year	January 1	December 31
1	No	Sunday	Sunday
2	No	Monday	Monday
3	No	Tuesday	Tuesday
4	No	Wednesday	Wednesday
5	No	Thursday	Thursday
6	No	Friday	Friday
7	No	Saturday	Saturday
8	Yes	Sunday	Monday
9	Yes	Monday	Tuesday
10	Yes	Tuesday	Wednesday
11	Yes	Wednesday	Thursday
12	Yes	Thursday	Friday
13	Yes	Friday	Saturday
14	Yes	Saturday	Sunday

Calendars: 1899–2040

Year...Type	Year...Type	Year...Type	Year...Type	Year...Type	Year...Type
1899...1	1901...3	1929...3	1957...3	1985...3	2013...3
1900...2	1902...4	1930...4	1958...4	1986...4	2014...4
	1903...5	1931...5	1959...5	1987...5	2015...5
	1904...13	1932...13	1960...13	1988...13	2016...13
	1905...1	1933...1	1961...1	1989...1	2017...1
	1906...2	1934...2	1962...2	1990...2	2018...2
	1907...3	1935...3	1963...3	1991...3	2019...3
	1908...11	1936...11	1964...11	1992...11	2020...11
	1909...6	1937...6	1965...6	1993...6	2021...6
	1910...7	1938...7	1966...7	1994...7	2022...7
	1911...1	1939...1	1967...1	1995...1	2023...1
	1912...9	1940...9	1968...9	1996...9	2024...9
	1913...4	1941...4	1969...4	1997...4	2025...4
	1914...5	1942...5	1970...5	1998...5	2026...5
	1915...6	1943...6	1971...6	1999...6	2027...6
	1916...14	1944...14	1972...14	2000...14	2028...14
	1917...2	1945...2	1973...2	2001...2	2029...2
	1918...3	1946...3	1974...3	2002...3	2030...3
	1919...4	1947...4	1975...4	2003...4	2031...4
	1920...12	1948...12	1976...12	2004...12	2032...12
	1921...7	1949...7	1977...7	2005...7	2033...7
	1922...1	1950...1	1978...1	2006...1	2034...1
	1923...2	1951...2	1979...2	2007...2	2035...2
	1924...10	1952...10	1980...10	2008...10	2036...10
	1925...5	1953...5	1981...5	2009...5	2037...5
	1926...6	1954...6	1982...6	2010...6	2038...6
	1927...7	1955...7	1983...7	2011...7	2039...7
	1928...8	1956...8	1984...8	2012...8	2040...8

GLOSSARY INDEX

A
Addition, 6, 7, 25
Algebra
 negative sign, 6, 19
 ordered pairs, 3
 positive sign, 6, 19
 timeline, 3
Analysis, 13, 19, 22, 44
Arithmetic, 25
Average, 6
 income, 7
 number, 19

B
Balance, 7
Base, 34
Base-ten, 1, 42
Budget, 5

C
Calculate, 2, 33, 34
Calculator, 5, 6, 7
Celsius, 33
Centuries, 16, 42, 45, 46
Circle, 20, 22, 37, 41
Columns, 7
Combination, 41
Commands, 3
Computer, 1, 2, 3, 30
 disks, 2
Corresponding, 14
Cubes
 number, 19, 20
Cycles, 1-47

D
Data, 1
 bank, 13, 43-47
Day, 14, 15, 16, 26, 31, 32, **33,** 36, 40, 41, 42, 45, 46 one revolution of Earth

Decades, 16, 45
Degrees, 33
Digits, 25
Divide, 7, 24, 38

E
Elapsed time, 3
Equal sign, 6
Estimate, 7
Expenditures, 4, 7 expenses

F
Fahrenheit, 33

G
Geometry, 2
 center, 2
 circle, 20, 22, 37, 41
 right angle, 40
Gigabytes, 24
Greatest number, 19

H
Hours, 16, 18, 23, 32, 33, 40, 45

I
Inch, 3
Income, 4, 7 earnings
 average, 7
Integers, 19
Isometric dot paper, 30

K
Kilograms, 33
Kilometers, 33

L
Leap year, 14, 26, 45, 47
Least number, 22
Least positive number, 38
Lengths, 3, 32, 33

Linear, 33
Liters, 33

M
Mathematics toolkit, 4-12
Measurement, 32, 33, 45-47
 base-ten, 42
 Celsius, 33
 centuries, 16, 42, 45, 46
 days, 14, 15, 16, 26, 31, 32, 33, 36, 40, 42, 45, 46
 decades, 16, 45
 degrees, 33
 Fahrenheit, 33
 gigabytes, 24
 hours, 16, 18, 23, 32, 33, 40, 45
 inch, 3
 kilograms, 33
 kilometers, 33
 leap year, 14, 26, 45, 47
 length, 3, 32, 33
 linear, 33
 liters, 33
 meters, 33
 metric, 42
 metric days, 31
 metric hours, 31
 metric miniseconds, 31
 metric minutes, 31
 metric months, 31
 metric seconds, 31
 metric units, 33
 metric week, 31
 metric year, 31
 miles, 33
 milliseconds, 45
 minutes, 15, 16, 18, 27, 33, 39, 40, 45
 months, 6, 7, 16, 23, 32, 33, 45, 46
 nanoseconds, 45
 per-piece costs, 2
 pounds, 33
 quarts, 33
 scores, 16, 45
 seasons, 16, 45
 seconds, 15, 16, 45

COVER: Scott Morgan/Westlight;